The kind of play that helps children most is play that really engages the child. You may see this kind of engagement when your child is building with Lego blocks. He works hard to figure out ways to fit all the block people into the vehicle he has created. He sticks with the task, biting his tongue, and concentrating as he attempts to connect the blocks in just the way that he wants. He seems to have a plan in mind and focuses on accomplishing his mission. He's in the flow, not easily distracted, and solves problems as they arise without becoming frustrated or overwhelmed.

The persistence and stick-to-it-ness children demonstrate when engaged in such play helps them become better students. By improving their attention and focus through play experiences, children develop the skills they will need as schoolwork becomes more challenging. Also, future employers need workers who can carry out tasks to completion, as well as those who are innovative and come up with new ideas and applications. In fact, according to education experts, future employers in a "knowledge economy" want students to develop three important skills: critical thinking and problem-solving, the ability to communicate effectively, and the ability to collaborate (Friedman 2010). All three are developed as young children play in focused and productive ways.

What About Academic Learning?

> The children who thrive enter school with strong communication skills. They are confident and self-assured, adept at making friends, persistent, creative, and excited about learning. These are the qualities that children acquire through play (Segal 2004, 33).

High-level, engaging play also helps develop young children's academic skills—skills that will help them learn to read, write, and understand mathematics and science. For example, you may see your child pretend that each doll or stuffed animal has a name, role, voice, and distinct personality. She creates a story line and acts it out with the characters she created. She may use objects in unusual and interesting ways—a block may be a phone, a piece of cake, or a baby for the mama kitty. She has created her own world and is using her abstract thinking to keep her imagined story going for long periods of time.

Your child knows that what she is doing is not real. She is applying her understanding of people, relationships, personalities, and stories in a way that demands her brain to work abstractly. When she uses objects like the block to represent other things, she is using symbolic thinking. It's as if she is saying, "This block will symbolize a phone. I know it's not a real phone. I can step away from the reality and think in symbolic terms."

As children begin to understand the alphabet and learn that letters are symbols, they are also thinking abstractly. They will learn that certain combinations of letters create words that are symbols of things they have experienced. They will learn the combination of letters in the word *dog* means the same as the dearly beloved family pet. The same is true as children begin to recognize that numerals represent quantities. Pretend play prepares them to be better abstract, symbolic thinkers. So the more your child pretends, the better your child

Why Children PLAY

A Family Companion to
Developmentally Appropriate Play

Gaye Gronlund

The Purposes of This Brochure

This brochure has three purposes. It will help you

- identify the kind of play that helps your child most;
- recognize when your child gets the best play opportunities—at school, at child care, and at home;
- ensure your child has the best play experiences.

The Benefits of Engaging, High-Level Play

As children play, they are highly motivated to try new things, gain knowledge and understanding, acquire and practice skills, and apply concepts. Now, researchers from fields other than education (pediatrics, evolutionary biology, neuroscience and mental health) are supporting the importance and benefits of play for children's optimal development. These researchers are raising serious concerns about trends in child rearing and education that are decreasing how much young children play. They advocate that play needs to be more of a focus in family life, preschool, and kindergarten.

> We believe that the stifling of play has dire consequences—not only for children but for the future of our nation. . . . No human being can achieve his full potential if his creativity is stunted in childhood. And no nation can thrive in the 21st century without a highly creative and innovative workforce. Nor will democracy survive without citizens who can form their own independent thoughts and act on them (Miller and Almon 2009, 1–2).

will be at making sense of letters, words, numerals, and mathematical symbols.

Scientific thinking is based on testing hypotheses. Scientists continually question what will happen with different variables and then set up experiments to test their ideas. That's exactly what young children do as they play. They are testing hypotheses, such as "I wonder what will happen if I put this big heavy block on top of my tower of smaller blocks? Boom! Down it fell. Will it happen if I do it again? What if I put a small block on top of my tower? Then will it stand?" This kind of experimentation prepares children to be better students, not only in science, as they develop critical thinking and are able to make predictions based on their experiences.

Finally, in many productive play experiences, children are required to regulate their impulses. For example, if two children sit next to each other and pretend to drive a car, only one child will handle the steering wheel and be the driver. The other child will act as the passenger. Both children know very well that there cannot be two drivers at the same time. They will regulate themselves to act out the driver and passenger roles so the play scenario can continue successfully. If the driver sits behind the passenger, the passenger may say, "You can't drive the car from the back. You have to sit in the front seat." When playing, children define their roles very clearly and regulate their own behavior to make them work.

> In play a child is always above his average age, above his daily behavior; in play it is as though he were a head taller than himself (Vygotsky 1976, 552).

Identifying High-Level Play

As a parent, you may be saying to yourself, "Yes, but . . . I've also seen times where my child was not very focused in his play. He roughhoused and was easily distracted. He jumped from toy to toy and never seemed to settle down." Or, "She sat in front of the television or computer screen for hours, staring blankly." Or, "He did the same thing over and over again. Is that what you mean by focused, engaged play?"

Your concerns are good ones. Not all children's play is beneficial or what researchers and educators describe as "high level." Children's play can easily disintegrate into silliness, roughhousing, lack of engagement, or inappropriate use of toys and materials. This is not the kind of play that helps children grow and learn. It's more of a free-for-all than an "in the flow" type of experience. Also, sitting in front of a screen (whether of a television or computer) is a form of passive engagement that doesn't demand the kind of active engagement of a child's thinking, imagination, and physical coordination that a high quality play experience involves. Trust your instincts. Here are ways to know when your child is engaged in productive play:

- Your child is highly engaged for extended periods of time, ranging anywhere from fifteen minutes to over one hour.
- When your child is playing with other children (siblings or friends), few behavior problems arise even though disagreements may have to be negotiated and compromises reached. But these negotiations are often quick and agreeable.
- The noise level is at a reasonable volume and can easily be quieted if necessary with a brief and friendly reminder.
- Adults or older siblings are called upon for specific needs such as to find an item that complements the play; to help settle a

disagreement; or to look, provide feedback, or affirmation. But then the play continues. The adult's continued involvement is not often needed.

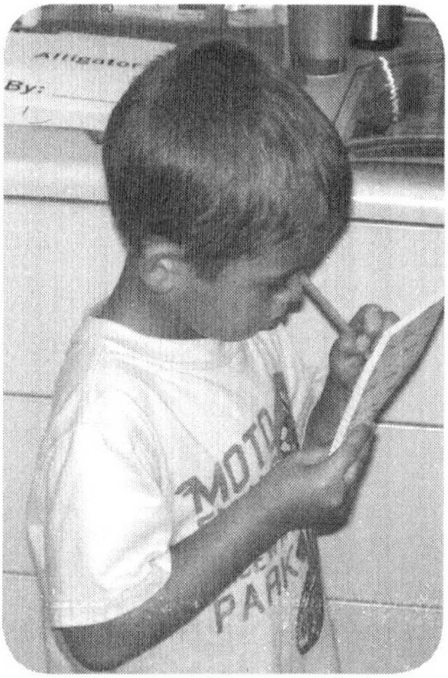

- Materials are used creatively. Real objects are not necessarily needed because a small block can be a cell phone or a stack of connecting cubes can serve as a fire hose.
- As your child plays with other children, they assign roles to each other and play out those roles within the general flow of the play scenario.

Play in Preschool and Kindergarten Classrooms

High-quality preschool and kindergarten programs include ample time for productive play to develop. Typically, the daily schedule includes one hour in the morning and one in the afternoon for play indoors, as well as time for children to play outdoors. Children can choose where they want to play, with whom, and for how long. The teachers plan for the materials and set up procedures that guide children's use of materials and interactions with each other. In addition, the teachers and caregivers do many things to help the children become engaged and stay engaged in high-level play. They provide additional items, make suggestions, listen to children's ideas, ask open-ended questions, and sometimes play alongside the children in order to get things started or to support in-depth play.

By interacting with children as they play, teachers are telling them, "What you're doing is important. I'm going to help you because I know your play is how you learn new skills and practice things you already know how to do." Children's intrinsic motivation to play is reinforced by teachers' involvement. Additionally, teachers can steer the play back on track if it begins to disintegrate from the high-level, focused, and productive engagement that is the goal.

Play at Home

You can do the very same things at home. By showing interest in what your child is doing— asking questions, making suggestions, and listening to your child's explanations and ideas—you, too, are telling your child how important his thinking and imagination are to you. You can take on roles in pretend stories, acting out characters or drinking invisible tea from an empty cup. To make the play more fun, you can suggest new ideas or help get household materials, like cardboard paper towel rolls, ribbons, or fabric scraps. While fixing dinner, invite your child to play at the table and engage him in a conversation about what he's building or what he is drawing. Houschold tasks such as folding laundry can be made playful too. "Where do you think the other brown sock is? Where are you brown sock? Brown sock, brown sock. Where are you brown sock? Oh, here you are! Now, can you find the white one with the red stripe?"

The Play Belongs to the Child

It's important for adults to be involved in children's play—and it's a tricky business. Most of the time, the direction of the play should be determined by the child—not the teacher or parent. The adult watches the play to determine if the child successfully furthers the play scenario, or if the child needs the adult to step in and take the lead for a short time to enhance the play. But the adult quickly steps out again, turning the lead back over to the child.

Adults also need to be careful when making comments or asking questions about a child's play. Timing is important; sometimes our best intentions actually interrupt what is happening. The goal of questions or comments is to facilitate the play, to help it move to or sustain a higher level. Well-timed questions can encourage children to think, problem solve, try a different approach, incorporate symbolic materials, or develop new play themes. If done well, children show greater interest in their play. However, poorly timed questioning can turn children off. It's an interruption. It stops the flow of the play and makes it less fun and enjoyable.

Supportive, interested adults can enhance play experiences for children and help them sustain a high level of engagement. In most circumstances, it's best to ask open-ended questions like "What do you think will happen if you . . . ?" or "What ideas do you have to solve that problem?" You can also make encouraging comments like "Wow, you used a lot of blocks to build that bridge." The children will let you know by their continued engagement that your involvement is welcome. The best thing an adult can hear from a child is "Look what I did!" That's a clear invitation to get involved and support the child in what she is doing.

This is a family companion to *Developmentally Appropriate Play: Guiding Young Children to a Higher Level* by Gaye Gronlund. Gaye is an early childhood consultant who trains early childhood educators across the country. She is a former preschool, kindergarten, and primary teacher of both regular and special education and holds a master's degree in adult learning and early childhood education.

Published by Redleaf Press
10 Yorkton Court
St. Paul, MN 55117
www.redleafpress.org

ISBN 978-1-60554-102-0

Redleaf Press®
www.redleafpress.org
800-423-8309